Bounce! Bounce!

Do you know the name of this jumping animal?

This animal
is a
kangaroo.

Most kangaroos live in *Australia.*

But they do not all live in the same part of Australia.

Some kangaroos live in forests or grassy places.

Other kangaroos live in high, rocky places.

These kangaroos spend a lot of time in trees.

These are red kangaroos. They are the largest type of kangaroo.

Red kangaroos live mostly in wide-open spaces called *plains*.

The plains of Australia are hot and dry.

How do red kangaroos stay cool?

Red kangaroos lick their front legs.
The wetness cools their skin.

What else
do they do?

Red kangaroos sleep during the
hottest part of the day.

A red kangaroo digs a hole in the cool ground for sleeping.

The hole fits the kangaroo just right.

Kangaroos look for food during the cooler parts of the day.

Red kangaroos mostly eat dry grasses.

Sometimes red kangaroos find water to drink.

But these kangaroos can go a long time without water.

Listen! Do you hear something?
This kangaroo hears a *predator.*

A predator is an animal that hunts and eats other animals.

This predator is called a dingo.

These red kangaroos are hopping
away from a predator.

A hopping kangaroo moves both
back legs together.

The strong back legs of a kangaroo help it hop fast.

A kangaroo tucks in its shorter front legs.

Red kangaroos live and travel in groups. A group of red kangaroos is called a *mob*.

A mob has mothers, fathers, and baby kangaroos.

Baby kangaroos are called *joeys*. Where is a joey born?

A joey is born in a *pouch* attached to its mother's belly.

The pouch is warm and soft.

Animals born in pouches are called *marsupials*.

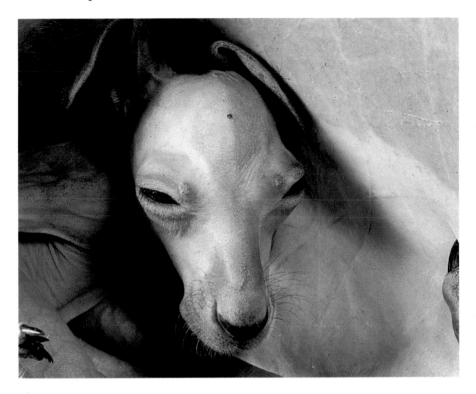

The pouch of a kangaroo is a safe place for a growing joey.

This joey wants to see the world.
It pops its head out of the pouch.

A joey can climb in and out of its mother's pouch.

After about eight months, the joey comes out for good.

The young kangaroo learns to jump and look for food.

It learns to watch for predators.

One day, it will be a big red kangaroo!

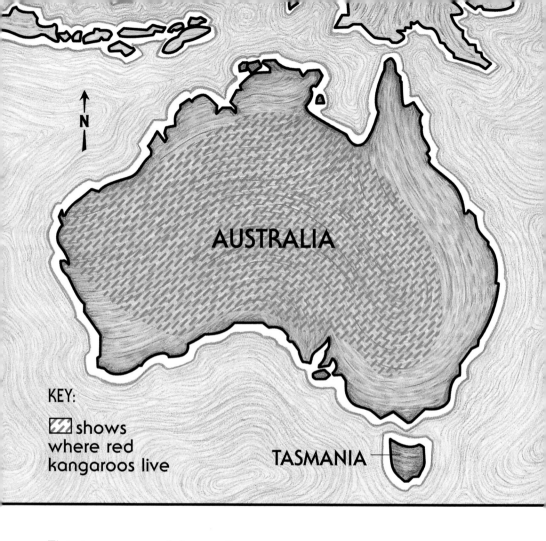

KEY:

shows where red kangaroos live

AUSTRALIA

TASMANIA

This is a map of Australia.

Where do red kangaroos live?

Parts of a Red Kangaroo

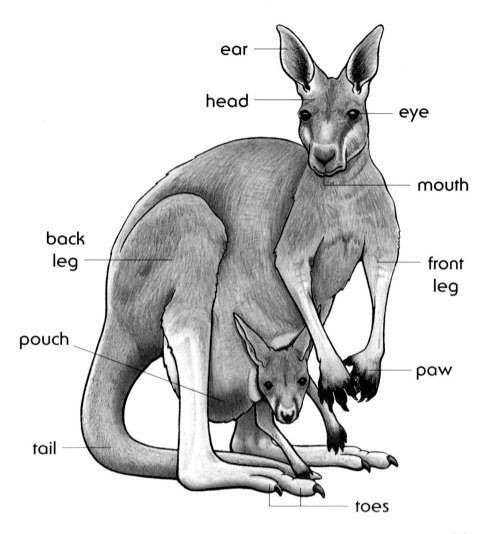

ear

head

eye

mouth

back leg

front leg

pouch

paw

tail

toes

29

Glossary

Australia: a large country in the southern half of the planet

joeys: baby kangaroos

marsupials: animals that are born and grow up in their mothers' pouches

mob: a group of kangaroos that live together

plains: land where there are wide-open spaces and very few trees

pouch: a warm, furry sack attached to a mother kangaroo's belly. A baby kangaroo is born in the pouch.

predator: an animal that hunts and eats other animals

Hunt and Find

- a kangaroo **digging a hole** on page 13
- a kangaroo **eating** dry grass on page 14
- a kangaroo **licking its front legs** on page 11
- a kangaroo **listening** for a predator on page 16
- kangaroos **jumping** on pages 3, 18, 19 and 27

About the Author

Michelle Levine is an author and editor. She lives in St. Paul, Minnesota.

Photo Acknowledgments

The photos in this book are reproduced through the courtesy of:
© Tom Brakefield/CORBIS, front cover; © Hans & Judy Beste/Lochman Transparencies, pp. 3, 8; © Martin Harvey/ANTphoto.com, p. 4;
© Jean-Paul Ferrero/AUSCAPE, pp. 5, 11, 12, 13, 14, 18, 19, 21, 22, 23, 24, 25, 26, 27; © Jay Sarson/Lochman Transparencies, p. 6;
© Jiri Lochman/Lochman Transparencies, p. 7; © Dave Watts/ANT photo.com, p. 9; © Tony Howard/ANTphoto.com, p. 10; © Nicholas Birks/AUSCAPE, p. 15; © Otto Rogge/ANTphoto.com, p. 16; © Dennis Sarson/Lochman Transparencies, pp. 17, 31; © Carlyn Galati/Visuals Unlimited, p. 20.